When I Am Afraid

WRITTEN BY

Sally Michael

ILLUSTRATED BY

Nicole Manuel

When I Am Afraid

© 2018 by Next Generation Resources, Inc. Illustrations by Truth78.

All rights reserved. No part of this publication may be reproduced in any form without written permission from Truth78.

Published in Minneapolis, Minnesota by Truth78.

All Scripture quotations, unless otherwise noted, are from the ESV® Bible (The Holy Bible, English Standard Version®) copyright © 2011 by Crossway, a publishing ministry of Good News Publishers. Used by permission. All rights reserved. ESV Text Edition: 2016.

ISBN-13: 978-0-9969869-2-2

Truth:78 / Equipping the Next Generations to Know, Honor and Treasure God

Truth78.org · info@Truth78.org · 877.400.1414 · @Truth78org

This book was inspired by

Rita Spidel

*who wanted her grandson to hear the
teaching from God's Word that puts
our fears in the right perspective.*

This book is dedicated to

Aaron and Jennifer Pettersen

*and their four children,
Isaac, Sara Jo, Luke, and John David.*

*May you always fear the Lord but stand fearless before those
"who kill the body but cannot kill the soul."*

*May you be faithful witnesses of your Lord regardless of the cost
as you look toward your eternal reward.*

*Thank you for your partnership
in discipling the next generation.*

A WORD TO PARENTS

It is not uncommon for children to experience fear—some fears being reasonable and others unfounded. Things that go "bump" in the night, big dogs, being in a strange place among strangers, and even climbing to the top of a slide or monkey bars can produce anxiety in children. Reasoning with a child about his fears, or simply telling him "not to be afraid" is most often ineffective. So how do parents help children with their fears?

Children need the confidence that there is someone bigger, stronger, and wiser than themselves who will protect and care for them. But more than that, they need the assurance that someone will be there for them—to make everything right, to handle the difficulties they can't, to accomplish the tasks that are too hard for them, and to navigate the situations that are beyond their experience and ability. Often that bigger, stronger, wiser person is a parent; sometimes it is a grandparent or another adult.

But parents and other adults are not supreme, all-powerful, and all-knowing. Parents and other adults fail children and find situations they can't navigate well. Only One Person is sufficient to handle all the complexities of the universe and, in particular, the personal world of every child. That Person is God Almighty, the Creator and Ruler of all things.

There is *common* grace that God extends to all His creation and all His creatures. All people are recipients of God's goodness and care:

> ...For he makes his sun rise on the
> evil and on the good, and sends
> rain on the just and on the unjust.
> —Matthew 5:45b

God in His goodness and mercy provides a general care, protection, and provision for all people. This is *common* grace. Every child is a recipient of common grace. Every child can receive the assurance that there is a big God watching over the universe, keeping the earth in its orbit, holding the sun and stars in the sky, giving life and breathe to people, holding back the magnitude of evil Satan would inflict on mankind.

But there is a *particular grace* or *special grace* that God extends specifically to His children, those who have claimed Christ as their Savior and have put their confidence in Jesus and committed their lives to Him. To these His children, God has given marvelous and comforting promises. Promises like:

> My help comes from the LORD,
> who made heaven and earth.
> ³He will not let your foot be moved;
> he who keeps you will not slumber.

[4] Behold, he who keeps Israel will
neither slumber nor sleep.
—Psalm 121:2-4

"I will never leave you nor
forsake you."—Hebrews 13:5b

"My grace is sufficient for you,
for my power is made perfect in
weakness."—2 Corinthians 12:9

While every person experiences God's common grace—His love extended to all mankind—the specific promises of particular care and protection belong to the children of God. Look at the conditions associated with promises like these:

The name of the LORD is a strong
tower; the righteous man runs
into it and is safe.—Proverbs 18:10

For the eyes of the LORD
range throughout the earth to
strengthen those whose hearts
are fully committed to him.
—2 Chronicles 16:9a (NIV)[1]

The righteous? How can anyone truly be righteous? The human heart is latent with pride, selfishness, unkindness, envy, bitterness... and a multitude of other sinful attitudes. But Jesus' perfect righteousness—His perfect obedience to God's standards and right standing before God—is given to those who trust in Jesus for the forgiveness of their sins and turn away from their sins. This blessing of being acceptable to God is only made possible through the death and resurrection of Jesus.

Those who are trusting in Jesus and have committed their lives to Him are recipients of the particular promises in Scripture. Your child may or may not be in this category. For those who have entrusted their lives to Christ, there is great assurance in God's particular care for His children.

Regardless of your child's standing before God right now, you can assure your child that God is supreme, all-powerful, and all-knowing. You can encourage your child to put his trust in God and not in himself. You can show your child the wonderful promises of God and encourage him to look to God when he is fearful.

God in His mercy and grace extends His goodness to all who place their trust in Him. This book will show your child that God is trustworthy and that he must look beyond himself to the great God of the universe to give him courage, make him strong, and to help him handle life.

May God give you the grace and wisdom to encourage your child to turn to Him.

[1]This version is the NIV. ESV is: For the eyes of the LORD run to and fro throughout the whole earth, to give strong support to those whose heart is blameless toward him.—2 Chronicles 16:9a

HOW TO USE THIS BOOK

As you read this book, dialogue with your child as he is able. Look at the pictures, talk about fear in general, and ask about your child's particular fears. Help your child to identify and label what he is afraid of. Then show your child that though his resources are insufficient, God is unlimited. Nothing is too hard for Him. Point your child beyond himself to the all-sufficient sovereign Ruler of the Universe. Read the book often and talk about what is promised in the verses from the Bible. Help your child to understand and ponder the questions on the last page:

Have you told God you want to be His child?

**Do you trust in Him as your Helper, Refuge,
Hiding Place, and Protector?**

Can you say to Him, "You are my God"?

Encourage your child to memorize some of the verses—perhaps those which most specifically are helpful to his particular fears. Help your child to see that the great God of the Universe has made special promises that help us with our fears. These promises tell us that He cares, protects, and gives strength to those who trust Him. Lead him to pray, telling God about his fears, and praising God for His power, wisdom, and love.

Then, as your child experiences fear in everyday life, remind him of a promise. Encourage him to pray and trust God, and then face his fears in the strength that God provides. Learning to trust God is not an event but a process, so do not get discouraged if your child battles long and hard. Keep pointing him to God and His all-sufficiency.

Will you check under my bed?

Will you close the closet door?

Sometimes we are afraid.

Afraid of the dark.
Afraid of big dogs.
Afraid of new people.
Afraid of climbing high.

AFRAID

When I am afraid,
I put my trust
in You [God].

Psalm 56:3

God made the whole world
and everything in it.
He holds the sun and
the moon in place.

Lift up your eyes on high
and see: who created these?
He who brings out their
host by number,
calling them by name;
by the greatness of his might
and because he is strong in power,
not one is missing.

Isaiah 40:26

If God knows the name
of every single star
and never loses
even one of them,
can He take care of you?

My help comes from the LORD,
who made heaven and earth.
He will not let your foot be moved;
he who keeps you will not slumber.
Behold, he who keeps Israel
will neither slumber nor sleep.

PSALM 121:2-4

God is our refuge and strength,
a very present help in trouble.

PSALM 46:1

You are a hiding place for me;
you preserve me from trouble;
you surround me with
shouts of deliverance.

PSALM 32:7

It is always safe to go to God.
He is a Helper and a Protector
when things are hard.

The name of the LORD
is a strong tower;
the righteous man
runs into it and is safe.

PROVERBS 18:10

"I will never leave you
nor forsake you."

HEBREWS 13:5b

For the LORD will not
forsake his people;
he will not abandon
his heritage;

PSALM 94:14

"My grace
is sufficient for you,
for my power is made perfect
in weakness."

2 CORINTHIANS 12:9

If you trust in God,
you have His power to
help you when you are
weak or afraid
or think you can't
do something.

For the eyes of the LORD
range throughout the earth
to strengthen those whose hearts
are fully committed to him.

2 CHRONICLES 16:9a (NIV)*

*This version is the NIV. ESV is: For the eyes of the LORD run to and fro throughout the whole earth, to give strong support to those whose heart is blameless toward him.—2 CHRONICLES 16:9a

I will say to the LORD,
"My refuge and my fortress,
my God, in whom I trust."

PSALM 91:2

When I am afraid,
I put my trust in you.
In God, whose word I praise,
in God I trust;
I shall not be afraid.
What can flesh do to me?

PSALM 56:3-4

But I trust in You, O LORD;
I say, "You are my God."

PSALM 31:14

Have you told God
you want to be His child?

Do you trust in Him
as your Helper, Refuge,
Hiding Place, and Protector?

Can you say to Him,
"You are my God"?

Truth:78 / Equipping the Next Generations to Know, Honor, and Treasure God

Truth78 is a vision-oriented ministry for the next generations—that they may know, honor, and treasure God, setting their hope in Christ alone, so that they will live as faithful disciples for the glory of God.

Our mission is to nurture the faith of the next generations by equipping the church and home with resources and training that instruct the mind, engage the heart, and influence the will through proclaiming the whole counsel of God.

We are committed to developing resources and training that are God-centered, Bible-saturated, Gospel-focused, Christ-exalting, Spirit-dependent, doctrinally grounded, and discipleship-oriented.

RESOURCES AND TRAINING MATERIALS

Truth78 currently offers the following categories of resources and training materials:

VISION-CASTING AND TRAINING

We offer a wide variety of booklets, video and audio seminars, articles, and other practical training resources that highlight and further expound our vision, mission, and values, as well as our educational philosophy and methodology. Many of these resources are freely distributed through our website. These resources and trainings serve to assist ministry leaders, volunteers, and parents in implementing Truth78's vision and mission in their churches and homes.

CURRICULUM

We publish materials designed for formal Bible instruction. The scope and sequence of these materials reflects our commitment to teach children and youth the whole counsel of God over the course of their education. Materials include curricula for Sunday School, Midweek Bible programs, Backyard Bible Clubs or Vacation Bible School, and Intergenerational studies. Most of these materials can be adapted for use in Christian schools and education in the home.

PARENTING AND FAMILY DISCIPLESHIP

We have produced a variety of materials and training resources designed to help parents disciple their children. These include booklets, video presentations, family devotionals, children's books, articles, and other recommended resources. Furthermore, our curricula include Growing in Faith Together (GIFT) Pages to help parents apply what is taught in the classroom to their child's daily experience in order to nurture faith.

BIBLE MEMORY

Our Fighter Verses Bible memory program is designed to encourage churches, families, and individuals in the lifelong practice and love of Bible memory. The Fighter Verses program utilizes an easy-to-use Bible memory system with carefully chosen verses to help fight the fight of faith. For pre-readers, Foundation Verses features 76 key verses with simple images. Visit FighterVerses.com for weekly devotionals and free memory aids. Download the Fighter Verses App for quizzes, songs, devotionals, review reminders and other helps.

For more information on any of these resources and training materials contact:

Truth78.org · info@Truth78.org · 877.400.1414 · @Truth78org